W9-CCZ-159

Rock On! A Look at Geology

Outrageous Ores

Christine Petersen

ABDO Publishing Company

Printed in the United States of America, North Mankato, Minnesota.
092009
012011

 PRINTED ON RECYCLED PAPER

Cover Photo: Peter Arnold
Interior Photos: Alamy pp. 5, 24, 28; Andrew Silver/U.S. Geological Survey pp. 10, 12, 19;
    AP Images pp. 11, 25; Getty Images pp. 9, 21; iStockphoto pp. 8, 15, 26, 27;
    Jupiterimages pp. 6, 29; National Geographic Image Collection p. 7; Peter Arnold pp. 1, 8, 13, 15;
    Photo Researchers p. 23

Series Coordinator: Megan M. Gunderson
Editors: Heidi M.D. Elston, Megan M. Gunderson
Art Direction & Cover Design: Neil Klinepier

Library of Congress Cataloging-in-Publication Data

Petersen, Christine.
  Outrageous ores / Christine Petersen.
    p. cm. -- (Rock on! A look at geology)
  Includes index.
  ISBN 978-1-60453-745-1
  1. Ores--Juvenile literature. 2. Mineralogy--Juvenile literature. I. Title.
  QE390.P48 2010
  553--dc22
                          2009033791

Contents

Sutter's Mill

In 1839, John Sutter was one of the few settlers of the California wilderness. He was soon granted a huge area of land. In time, Sutter needed more lumber for building. So, he asked carpenter James Wilson Marshall to set up a sawmill.

For the mill, Marshall chose a spot along the American River. The mill required a steady source of water to run. So, Marshall's workers dug two deep channels. These would bring water from the river to the mill and back again.

On January 24, 1848, Marshall went out to check on the lower channel. That day, something in the water caught his eye. "I reached my hand down and picked it up," he later recalled. "It made my heart thump, for I was certain it was gold."

Without planning it, the workers at Sutter's Mill had struck an ore. An ore is an **aggregation** of one or more minerals that can be mined for profit. In Marshall's case, that valuable mineral was gold!

Marshall's gold came from a placer deposit. An ancient stream caused it to collect there. Over millions of years, the gold was buried. When Marshall's workers dug into the ground and the water flowed over, they brought the gold back into the sunlight!

Sutter's Mill

5

A Special Recipe

Have you ever made a giant cookie? Flour, sugar, eggs, butter, and more get mixed together. Then, the recipe calls for chocolate chips. After they're stirred in, the batter is spread out across a pan and baked.

Now, imagine taking a close look at the cookie before eating it. Can you spot a few chips? You could easily pick out these goodies. But where have the other ingredients gone? They are mixed together throughout the cookie. Did you know your cookie is like Earth's rocks and minerals?

Earth is covered in a layer of rock called the crust. Rocks are made up of minerals. Minerals are solid, nonliving substances that form naturally on Earth.

Like the chips in your cookie, ore minerals are always surrounded by other minerals.

Most rocks are made up of more than one kind of mineral. Often, these ingredients are well mixed. You'd find it hard to collect just one kind. Yet in some areas, rocks contain clumps of a specific mineral. Like the chips in your cookie, they are easier to locate and mine.

These unusually high amounts of a specific mineral are called mineral deposits. This is a geologic term. Mineral deposits have been discovered around the world. If one can be mined at a profit, it is called an ore deposit. That is an **economic** term.

All ore deposits are mineral deposits. But, not all mineral deposits are ore deposits. To be ore deposits, they must be profitable to mine.

Mineral Building Blocks

Quartz

Gold

    At a museum's mineral exhibit, you might see examples of gold and quartz. Gold looks like a shiny, yellow blob. Quartz crystals resemble small, white skyscrapers. You would never mix up these two minerals on a test!

    Yet under a microscope, gold and quartz have something in common. Both are made from tiny building blocks called atoms. These make up **elements**.

    Scientists have identified more than 90 different elements in nature. Every mineral contains at least one. For example, gold is made up of gold atoms. Many minerals contain more than one **element**. Quartz has atoms of the elements silicon and oxygen.

Different minerals have different combinations of elements. Scientists have discovered about 3,000 minerals. Only about 100 are considered ore minerals. Most of these are the source of useful or valuable metals.

Quartz often occurs with large gold deposits.

Making Minerals

Minerals form in several ways. In some cases, the way they form causes them to become concentrated. Then, they may be called mineral deposits.

Some minerals form from cooling **magma**. It flows upward from below Earth's crust. It may reach the surface and spread across the ground as lava. This cools quickly, which does not give mineral grains much time to grow.

Magma that remains trapped underground cools very slowly. Under these conditions, larger mineral grains may form. In some cases, this slow cooling leads to mineral deposits.

For example, the ore mineral chromite can form deposits in cooling magma. It is very **dense**. So, it sinks as it forms. This means lots of chromite ends up in the same place. It is an ore of the metal chromium.

Chromite (right) is a source of chromium. Chromium is combined with other metals to make products as different as forks and car bumpers!

Chromite is mined in such areas as India (above) *and South Africa.*

Water can also form mineral deposits. Hot **magma** releases some of this water. Other water trickles down from Earth's surface. It flows deep underground through tiny spaces in rock. Along the way, it collects various **elements** and minerals.

To form a deposit, the water must be affected by its surroundings in some way. Water entering an open space in rock may boil, cool, or react with surrounding rock. This causes the water to deposit its load of minerals. Copper deposits often form because of water.

On Earth's surface, rocks are continually worn down. Flowing surface water picks up rock pieces. It breaks them down and concentrates them somewhere else. This leads to placer deposits, such as the one at Sutter's Mill.

Lakes and oceans carry minerals, too. The minerals settle out of the water to form sediment layers. Deposits of the mineral hematite form this way. It is an important iron ore.

Hematite can be red in color. Its name comes from the Greek word for "blood."

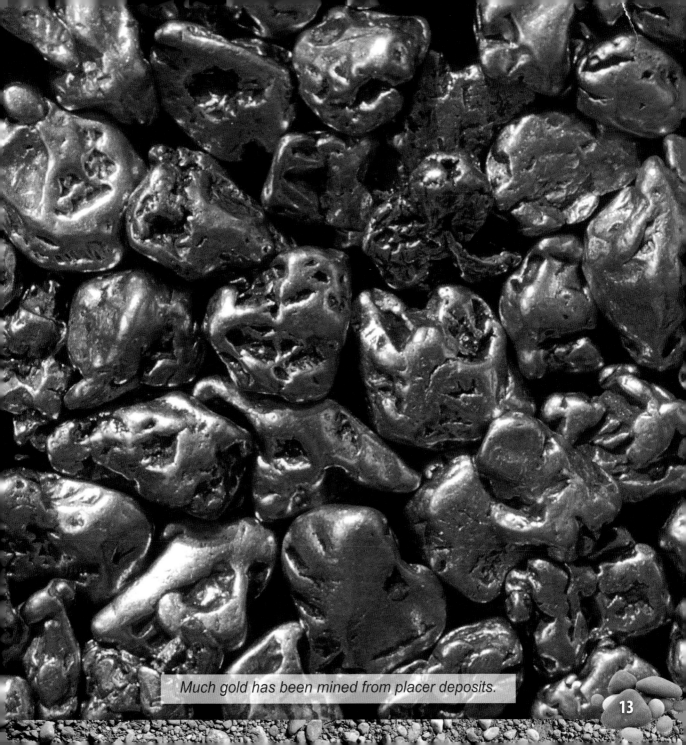

Much gold has been mined from placer deposits.

Amazing Metals

Most ore minerals are mined for the important metals they contain. Metals are shiny and can be shaped easily. They conduct heat and electricity. Metals can be strong and long lasting, especially when combined.

Metals are found in things you use every day. They are in cars, batteries, jewelry, tools, and baseball bats. Do you have a bicycle? It may contain the lightweight metal titanium. Inside your computer, copper helps things run. Look around to find other examples in your home and school. All of these metals came from ores.

The metals we use fit into two classes. They can be **geochemically** abundant or scarce. The five abundant metals are aluminum, iron, magnesium, manganese, and titanium. They are found in many common rocks. All other metals are scarce. They include copper, lead, gold, and silver.

To meet the need for metals, huge amounts of ore must be mined each year. In 2008, almost 60 million tons (54 t) of iron ore were mined in the United States. That's about the weight of 160 Empire State Buildings! Yet, it was only 3 percent of the iron ore produced and used worldwide.

Metals are part of our everyday lives.

Mine Your Cereal!

What You'll Need

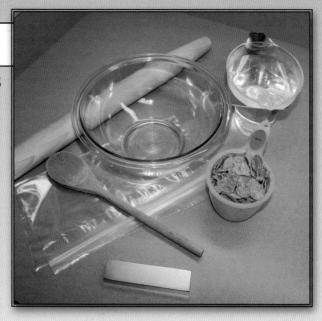

- 1 cup iron-fortified cereal flakes
- resealable plastic bag
- rolling pin
- bowl
- 2 cups hot water
- wooden spoon
- magnet (not black)

What You'll Do

1. Put the cereal in the plastic bag and seal it.

2. Use the rolling pin to crush the cereal.

3. Pour the crushed cereal into your bowl.

4. Add the hot water to the bowl.

5. Using your wooden spoon, stir until the cereal breaks down. It will get very mushy!

6. Now, stir the mixture with your magnet for a couple of minutes.

7. Pull the magnet out of the cereal slush. Look carefully. Are there little black bits stuck to the magnet? That is the iron from your cereal!

2

4

6

Clean magnet

7

17

Classifying Ores

Minerals are grouped based on the **elements** they contain. Of the 11 groups, five contain preferred ore minerals. They are native metals, silicates, carbonates, sulfides, and oxides and hydroxides.

Gold and platinum often occur in their native state. That means these metals are not combined with other elements. Silver and copper may also occur this way.

Silicate minerals contain the elements silicon and oxygen, and often a metal element. In this group is garnierite, an ore of nickel. Nickel can be combined with other metals to make stainless steel. All carbonates contain carbon and oxygen. Rhodochrosite is in this group. As an ore, it is a major source of manganese.

Sulfide minerals combine metals with sulfur. They make up the largest group of ore minerals. Galena is the main ore of lead. Cinnabar is the main source of mercury. Telluride minerals are a special type of sulfide. They each contain the element tellurium and a valuable metal.

Oxides and hydroxides are the last group. Bauxite is the main ore of aluminum. Rutile and ilmenite are sources of the metal titanium. This metal is lightweight and resists heat. So, it is often used in airplane construction.

Bauxite

Let's Explore!

Mining ores is expensive and takes a long time. That's why companies prospect and explore before starting to dig. Prospecting is the search for a mineral deposit.

Modern science makes prospecting easier. Special **satellite** cameras find some minerals. Magnets help find minerals such as magnetite, an iron ore.

Once found, a mineral deposit is explored to determine its worth. The ultimate goal is to find an ore body. This is a deposit with clear boundaries that contains minerals that can be mined for profit.

Several factors determine whether a deposit is worth mining. One of these is grade. This is a measure of how much of a deposit is valuable minerals and how much is **gangue**. The less gangue there is, the higher the grade. A high-grade deposit is more likely to be profitable.

Before opening a mine, companies also consider how much they can sell the ore for. They compare this with the cost to remove and process it. And, they see if too much of the same metal is already available. If so, it may be wiser to mine it at a later time.

Other factors include how big and what shape the deposit is. The deposit's location also affects how easily and cheaply it can be mined. Exploring helps determine all of these factors.

Drilling into a mineral deposit for samples helps geologists determine its grade.

In the Pit

Mining can begin once an ore body has been discovered. One place this has happened is El Chino in New Mexico. From a distance, you might mistake this mine for a canyon.

Looking into the mine, you can tell this is actually the work of humans. The rock has been cut away in layers that dip deep into the earth. This makes it look like a huge stadium. Yet no games will ever be played there. El Chino is an open-pit copper mine.

An open-pit copper mine is a busy place! The miners start by blasting away sections of rock to obtain the ore. Large trucks then carry away the broken pieces. They must be processed to obtain the copper.

For much copper ore, the first step is to crush the ore. These tiny bits are then soaked in water. **Gangue** falls to the bottom, while copper floats to the top. Next, the metal is melted and separated from any other minerals. In the end, nearly pure copper is all that remains.

Open-pit mining is just one type of surface mining. Strip mining is a similar way to remove ores. Miners remove strips of earth one at a time. Waste from each new strip is left in the old strip next to it. Quarrying is the removal of stone in specific shapes, sizes, and qualities. Mountaintop removal is mainly for mining coal, which is used as a fuel.

An open-pit copper mine

Digging Deep

The price of a metal can increase. Then, deposits that were once too deep may become worth mining.

Many ore deposits are found too deep for surface mining. In these cases, underground mines are dug. From there, ores must be carried to the surface for processing.

The world's deepest mines are in South Africa. Gold was discovered there in Witwatersrand in the 1880s. The area contains the largest single gold ore body in the world. That makes it a bonanza! More than 40 percent of the gold ever mined in the world comes from this area.

Even the biggest bonanza can't last forever. Still, mining companies in South Africa have begun planning deeper and deeper mines. To reach good ores, one mine will reach more than two miles (3 km) underground.

Even after a mine opens, companies continue to think about profits. They compare the value of the ore to the cost of mining. A mine may close if sale of the ore will be less than the cost to produce it. Or, a mine may close when an ore body is used up.

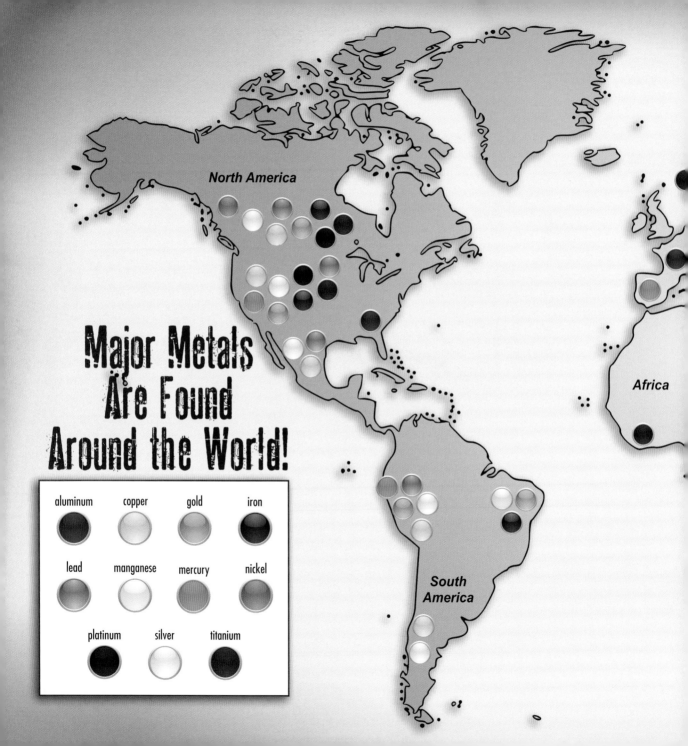

Major Metals Are Found Around the World!

North America

Africa

South America

aluminum	copper	gold	iron
lead	manganese	mercury	nickel
platinum	silver	titanium	

Europe

Asia

Australia

N

W   E

S

Ores in Our Lives

People have been mining minerals for thousands of years. Early on, they used native metals such as gold and copper. They shaped them into practical and beautiful objects. Today, we know how to obtain metals from many different ores.

Ores are one of the most important **natural resources** on Earth. Metals are everywhere in our lives. And, mining provides many different jobs for people around the world.

Yet there is a price for using these resources. Natural **habitats** must be cleared to

Restoring land is an important step in the mining process.

Recycling is an easy way to help the planet.

open some mines. And, mining can cause pollution. So, laws exist to reduce damage to the **environment**.

Mining companies know it is important to protect nature and people. One helpful step they can take is to fill in a mine after it closes. Replacing trees and ground cover helps natural **habitats** grow back.

Once an ore is removed from the earth, it can never be replaced. But, we can all do our part to make sure metal isn't wasted. Learn about recycling programs in your community. It's possible to turn your old soda can into a new one. Together, we can protect Earth's **natural resources**.

Glossary

aggregation - a group, body, or mass made up of many distinct parts or individuals.

dense - having a high mass per unit volume.

economic - relating to the production and use of goods and services.

element - any of the more than 100 simple substances made of atoms of only one kind.

environment - all the surroundings that affect the growth and well-being of a living thing.

gangue - worthless minerals mixed in with valuable minerals.

geochemically - relating to the chemical and geological properties of something.

habitat - a place where a living thing is naturally found.

magma - melted rock beneath Earth's surface.

natural resource - a material found in nature that is useful or necessary to life. Water, forests, and minerals are examples of natural resources.

satellite - a manufactured object that orbits Earth. It relays scientific information back to Earth.

Saying It

bauxite - BAWK-site
gangue - GANG
garnierite - GAHR-nee-uh-rite
ilmenite - IHL-muh-nite
manganese - MANG-guh-neez
placer - PLA-suhr
rhodochrosite - roh-duh-KROH-site
telluride - TEHL-yuh-ride
Witwatersrand - WIHT-waw-tuhrz-rand

Web Sites

To learn more about ores, visit ABDO Publishing Company on the World Wide Web at **www.abdopublishing.com**. Web sites about ores are featured on our Book Links page. These links are routinely monitored and updated to provide the most current information available.

Index